Quit It!

by Marie Powell

illustrated by Amy Cartwright

Ideas for Parents and Teachers

Amicus Readers let children practice reading at early reading levels. Familiar words and concepts with close illustration-text matches support early readers.

Before Reading

- Discuss the cover illustration with the child. What does it tell him?
- Ask the child to predict what she will learn in the book.

Read the Book

- "Walk" through the book and look at the illustrations. Let the child ask questions.
- Point out the colored words. Ask the child what is the same about them (spelling, ending sound).
- Read the book to the child, or have the child read to you.

After Reading

- Use the word family list at the end of the book to review the text.
- Prompt the child to make connections. Ask: *What other words end with -it?*

Amicus Readers are published by Amicus
P.O. Box 1329, Mankato, MN 56002
www.amicuspublishing.us

Library of Congress Cataloging-in-Publication Data
Powell, Marie, 1958-
  Quit it! / Marie Powell.
    pages cm. -- (Word families)
  K to Grade 3.
  Audience: Age 6
  ISBN 978-1-60753-584-3 (hardcover) --
  ISBN 978-1-60753-650-5 (pdf ebook)
1. Reading--Phonetic method. 2. Reading (Primary) I. Title.
LB1573.3.P6958 2014
372.46'5--dc23
                          2013044009

Illustrations by Amy Cartwright

Produced for Amicus by The Peterson Publishing Company and Red Line Editorial.

Editor Jenna Gleisner
Designer Craig Hinton
Printed in the United States of America
Mankato, MN
9/2014
P01228
10 9 8 7 6 5 4 3 2

Kit is my little sister.

She gets on my nerves.

I always tell her, "Quit it!"

In the car, Kit won't sit still. She likes to hit her toy drum all the way to the store.

"Quit it!" I say.

At home, I practice my skit for dance class. But Kit is wearing my outfit.
"Quit it!" I say.

Next, Kit steals my drawing. When she picks it up, she tears a slit in it. "Quit it!" I say.

We play outside. Kit jumps in a puddle. Mud lands on my knit scarf.

"Quit it!" I say.

At snack time, I split my apple with Kit. Kit takes one of my slices. She bites into it.

"Quit it!" I say.

I let **Kit** keep the slice she **bit**. But I ask her to **quit** taking my slices.

"Fine, I'll **quit it!**" says Kit.

Word Family: -it

Word families are groups of words that rhyme and are spelled the same.

Here are the -it words in this book:

bit	quit
hit	sit
it	skit
Kit	slit
knit	split
outfit	

Can you spell any other words with -it?